Medicine stands still

CW00495957

Medieval medicine

1 **Tick the correct column to show if each belief about the causes of illness, effective protections and treatments is supernatural or natural.**

Beliefs about causes of illness, effective protections and treatments	Supernatural	Natural
God		
Bad smells or bad air		
Sinful lifestyle		
Childbirth		
Doctrine of signatures		
Warfare		
Famine		
Witchcraft		
Four humours out of balance		

2 **Complete the table to detail the work and impact of Hippocrates. The first row has been completed for you as an example.**

Hippocrates' work and ideas	Description	Impact on British medicine
Hippocratic oath	Doctors swear an oath to maintain high standards. It ensures their work is for the benefit of the patient and not for financial gain.	Had a long-term impact and a form of it is still used today.
Hippocratic collection		
Theory of four humours		
Observation and recording		

3 Complete the Venn diagram to show similarities and differences between the ideas and work of Hippocrates and Galen.

Two examples have been completed to help you get started.

You should also use the information from Question 2 to help you.

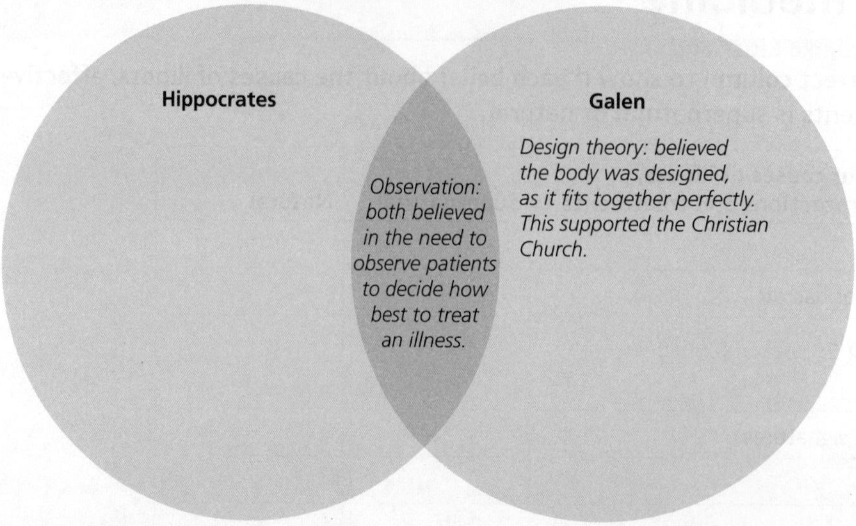

4 a **Complete the table to show who provided medical care in the Middle Ages.**

b **Colour code the treatments in the table to show the types of treatments used by each provider of medical care:**

- **Use blue to show natural treatments.**
- **Use yellow to show supernatural treatments.**

Provider of medical care	Training	How they treated the sick	Who would use the provider?
Physician			
Barber-surgeon			
Apothecary			
Wise woman			
Lady of the manor			

5 a Complete the diamond nine to show the extent to which the different factors listed below limited medical progress in medieval Britain. Place the factor which, in your opinion, limited progress the most at the top, working down to the factor with the least impact at the bottom.

Factors:

- i **Church**
- ii **Galenic ideas and techniques**
- iii **Hippocratic methods and treatments**
- iv **Lack of scientific understanding**
- v **Poor communication**
- vi **Basic technology**
- vii **Monasteries' control of education**
- viii **Conservatism**
- ix **Astrology**

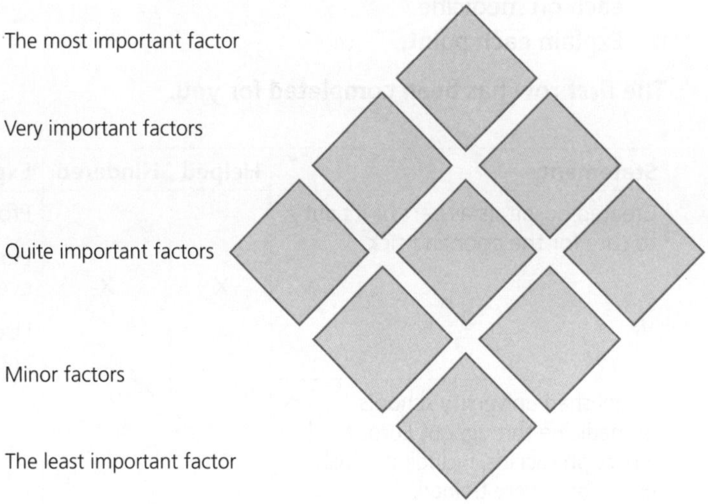

b Explain your top and bottom decision using specific examples.

Medical progress

6 **Read the statements about the Christian Church's impact on medicine during the Middle Ages.**

a **Place a cross in either the Helped or the Hindered column, or in both, to show the impact of each on medicine.**

b **Explain each point.**

The first row has been completed for you.

Statement	Helped	Hindered	Explanation
Created hospitals as part of its duty to care for the poor and sick.	X	X	Provided rest for those in need. Hospitals were very small and did not allow everyone to enter. Used prayer as a form of treatment in hospitals. Encouraged people to pray for forgiveness.
Established university schools of medicine throughout Europe where physicians, including British physicians, were trained.			
Taught the works of Galen because his ideas fitted with the design theory.			
Banned human dissection. This made it very hard for scholars to expand their knowledge or to question medical authors such as Galen.			
Some hospitals refused to treat the very sick or women.			
Monks translated texts from the Islamic world.			
Individuals such as Roger Bacon were accused of heresy. This was because they called for new approaches and original research.			

7 **Complete the table to show how the Islamic faith both progressed and hindered medicine during the Middle Ages. Add at least one more example to each column.**

Islamic faith progressed medicine	Islamic faith hindered medicine
Islamic ideas were brought back to Britain during the Crusades. Rhazes recorded the first accurate descriptions of smallpox.	Islamic law prevented dissection of the human body.

8 a Look at Source A. Label at least two different ways that care is being provided in this painting.

b Colour code your labels:

- Use yellow for evidence that supernatural treatments were used, for example prayer.
- Use blue for evidence that natural treatments were used, for example rest.

Source A

The Franciscans treating victims of the plague, miniature from an Italian manuscript produced in 1474

9 Define the following key surgical terminology.

- Cauterising: ....
- Amputation: ....
- Apprentice: ....
- Guild: ....
- Pus: ....
- Forceps: ....
- Infection: ....
- Ointment: ....

⑩ **Copy and complete the spider diagram to show different ways in which warfare helped surgery advance. The first two have been completed for you as examples.**

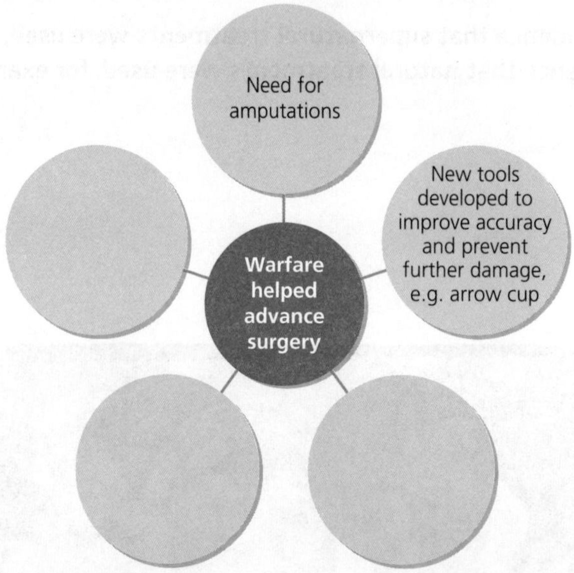

Public health in the Middle Ages

⑪ a **Copy and complete the spider diagram to create an overview of the Black Death in Britain, 1348–49. Add more circles with specific evidence.**

b **Colour code your points:**

- **Use green for evidence of scientific/natural beliefs and approaches.**
- **Use yellow for evidence of supernatural beliefs and approaches.**

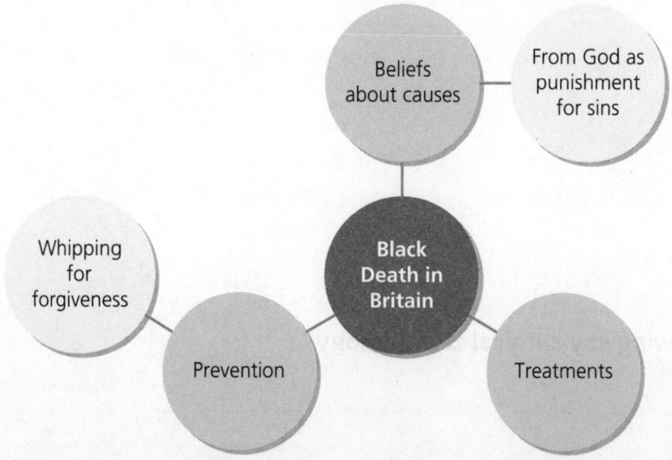

⑫ **Copy and complete the table, adding at least two examples on each side, to show the different ways in which monasteries helped and hindered public health during the Middle Ages.**

Monasteries helped progress public health	Monasteries hindered the advancement of public health
Created systems for fresh water.	Did not treat everyone who needed help nor did they allow certain illnesses to enter the monastery.

Exam-style questions

Source B

Blood-letting in the late thirteenth century

13 **How useful is Source B to a historian studying the treatments used by medieval practitioners?**

Explain your answer using Source B and your contextual knowledge. Answer this question on another sheet of paper and keep it with this workbook for reference. 10 **8 marks**

Tips for answering 'How useful is Source...' questions:

- **Evaluate the source based on its content (what you can see).**
- **Assess the usefulness based on the provenance of the source (authorship/date/purpose).**

14 **How useful is Source A (refer to Question 8 on page 7) to a historian studying treatments used by medieval practitioners?**

Explain your answer using Source A and your contextual knowledge. Answer this question on another sheet of paper and keep it with this workbook for reference. 10 **8 marks**

15 **How useful is the following paragraph to a historian studying ways people tried to prevent the Black Death?**

> In 1349 over six hundred men came to London from Flanders... Each wore a cap marked with a red cross in front and behind. Each had in his right hand a scourge with three tails. Each tail had a knot and through the middle of it there were sometimes sharp nails fixed. They marched naked in a file one behind the other and whipped themselves with these scourges on their naked bleeding bodies.

Robert of Avesbury, *Chronicle* (c.1360)

Explain your answer using the source and your contextual knowledge. Answer this question on another sheet of paper and keep it with this workbook for reference. 10 **8 marks**

16 **Explain the significance of the work of Hippocrates and Galen in the advancement of medicine.**

10 **8 marks**

Tips for answering 'Explain the significance of...' questions:

- **If two elements are mentioned, refer to both.**
- **For top marks, discuss both the short-term and long-term impacts.**

17 **Explain the significance of war in the advancement of surgery in the Middle Ages.**

10 **8 marks**

Two ideas to get you started:

- **John Arderne**
- **Development of new tools, including the arrow cup.**

The beginnings of change

The impact of the Renaissance on Britain

1 Complete the table to show the work of individuals on medicine during the Renaissance.

Individual	Area of medicine they challenged	How they challenged it	Opposition they faced
Vesalius	Anatomy		
Harvey		Proved the heart was a pump, challenging Galen who said the liver made blood.	
Paré			Surgeons did not like new ideas. They believed Paré's ligatures were too risky.

2 Read the statements about Thomas Sydenham.

a **Circle or highlight the facts about Sydenham that are accurate.**
b **Re-write all the inaccurate statements on the lines below.**

He believed in the need to examine and observe a patient before treatment was decided.	Sydenham believed in reading the works of ancient teachers such as Galen. He placed little value on experience.	He thought doctors should intervene and treat all patients.	Sydenham believed in exercise and moderation as a form of treatment.
Sydenham was refused a licence by the College of Physicians.	He was a strong advocate of the scientific approach and method in medicine.	Sydenham thought many diseases and illnesses were similar.	He developed the 'hot therapy'.

....

....

....

....

....

....

....

....

....

....

3 Explain the changes in status and training of surgeons during the Renaissance using the key words below.

- Apprenticeship
- Qualification
- Royal College of Surgeons
- Regulation
- Experience

....

....

....

....

....

....

Dealing with disease

4 Circle or highlight the statements about John Hunter that are correct.

Believed wounds healed best when left alone	Believed in the teachings of Galen	Dissected bodies to improve his knowledge of anatomy
Discovered antiseptics	Trained many of the best surgeons of his time	Dissected only animals to learn about the human body
Promoted the use of experimental research	Worked abroad most of his life	Was an army surgeon in France for a period of time

5 a Complete the spider diagram adding specific examples and details of treatments used in early modern Britain to each of the points.

b Highlight new treatments.

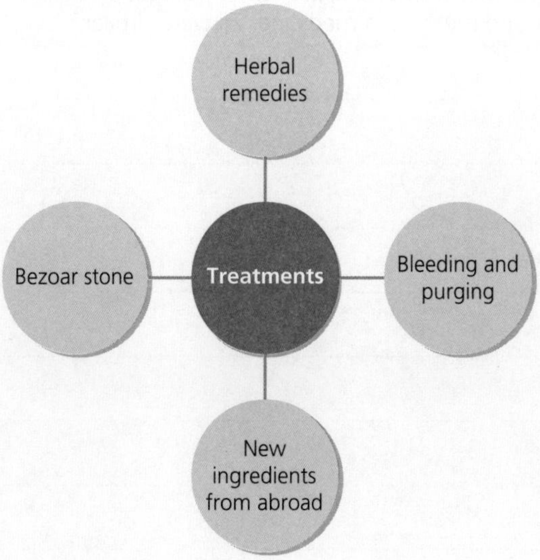

Source C

Great Plague of London (1665): the dead plague victims being collected and loaded on a cart during the 1665 plague epidemic in England

6 a Label key features of Source C.

b For each key feature make an inference about reactions to the Great Plague.

Prevention of disease

7 a Define 'inoculation'.

b Define 'vaccination'.

8 a **Put the events below in order to show how Edward Jenner discovered a vaccine for smallpox.**

b **Highlight where the following factors play a role:**

- **Use green for the role of government.**
- **Use blue for the use of a scientific approach.**

Event	Correct order
In 1796 Jenner injected James Phipps, a nine-year-old boy, with pus from the sores of Sarah Nelmes, a milkmaid with cowpox.	
Jenner submitted a paper to the Royal Society. It was refused, with a request for more evidence.	
Jenner continued to carry out more experiments, even on his own son.	
Jenner became aware that local milkmaids who caught cowpox never seemed to catch smallpox.	
Thomas Jefferson, the President of the United States, championed Jenner's work.	
In 1802 the British government awarded Jenner £10,000 for his work.	
In 1807 the Royal College of Physicians approved the vaccine, leading to the British government awarding Jenner a further £20,000.	
In 1798 Jenner published *An Inquiry into the Causes and Effects of the Variolae Vaccinae.*	
Phipps was immune to smallpox.	

9 **Give three specific pieces of evidence to prove there was opposition to Jenner's vaccination.**

1

2

3

10 **When did the British government make vaccination of children compulsory?**

....

11 **Give one reason why compulsory vaccination was ended.**

....

12 **Rank the individuals listed below on what you believe to be the impact of their ideas and work on the progress of medicine in Britain. Give specific reasons and short- and long-term impact.**

Individuals:

- **Andreas Vesalius**
- **Ambroise Paré**
- **William Harvey**
- **Thomas Sydenham**
- **Edward Jenner**

Rank order	Name	Reason
1		
2		
3		
4		
5		

13 The following factors are important in the Thematic Study. You must understand the impact of each on medicine. Complete the table to show the impact of each on medical progress during the Renaissance.

Remember: a factor can progress and/or hinder medicine.

Factor	Progressed medicine	Hindered medicine	Overall judgement from -5 to +5 (-5 = significantly hindered; 0 = no impact; +5 = significantly progressed)
Religion			
War			
Government			
Science and technology			
Role of the individual			

Exam-style questions

Source D

'Here you may be cured!' – a seventeenth-century quack doctor stands beside his counter, strewn with wonderful potions and elixirs to cure all ailments

14 **How useful is Source D to a historian studying attitudes towards medicine in the seventeenth century?**

Explain your answer using Source D and your contextual knowledge. 10 **8 marks**

15 **How useful is Source C (refer to Question 6 on page 13) to a historian studying methods used to prevent the Great Plague, 1665?**

Explain your answer using Source C and your contextual knowledge. 10 **8 marks**

Hint: Use your answers to Question 6 to help you plan your answer.

A revolution in medicine

The development of germ theory and its impact on the treatment of disease in Britain

1 Read the information in the table about Louis Pasteur and Robert Koch.

Code the boxes:

- **Use LP for the work of Louis Pasteur.**
- **Use RK for the work of Robert Koch.**

Discovered the germ theory in 1861.	Investigated and identified the bacterium that caused tuberculosis.	Developed a way to stain bacteria, making them easier to see under a microscope.
Work enabled other scientists to create vaccines to prevent human diseases.	While investigating anthrax, discovered the specific bacterium that causes it.	Created a vaccine against rabies.
Identified a method of proving a specific bacterium was causing a disease.	Discovered how Jenner's vaccine worked. Could now create other vaccines.	Following the death of his daughter and a cholera outbreak, started to investigate human disease.
Work enabled other scientists to find the specific bacteria for individual diseases.	Identified the bacterium causing chicken cholera.	Invented the process of pasteurisation.

2 Complete the table to show the impact of Paul Ehrlich's work on magic bullets and chemical treatments in Britain.

Describe the work of Ehrlich	Describe the short-term impact of Ehrlich's work	Describe the long-term impact of Ehrlich's work

3 a Rank these individuals according to who you believe had the greatest impact on medicine in Britain. Think about both short-term and long-term impacts.

- Louis Pasteur ☐
- Robert Koch ☐
- Paul Ehrlich ☐

b Explain why you placed your chosen individual at the top using specific evidence.

....

....

....

....

....

....

....

4 Complete the Venn diagram to show features of everyday treatments and remedies.

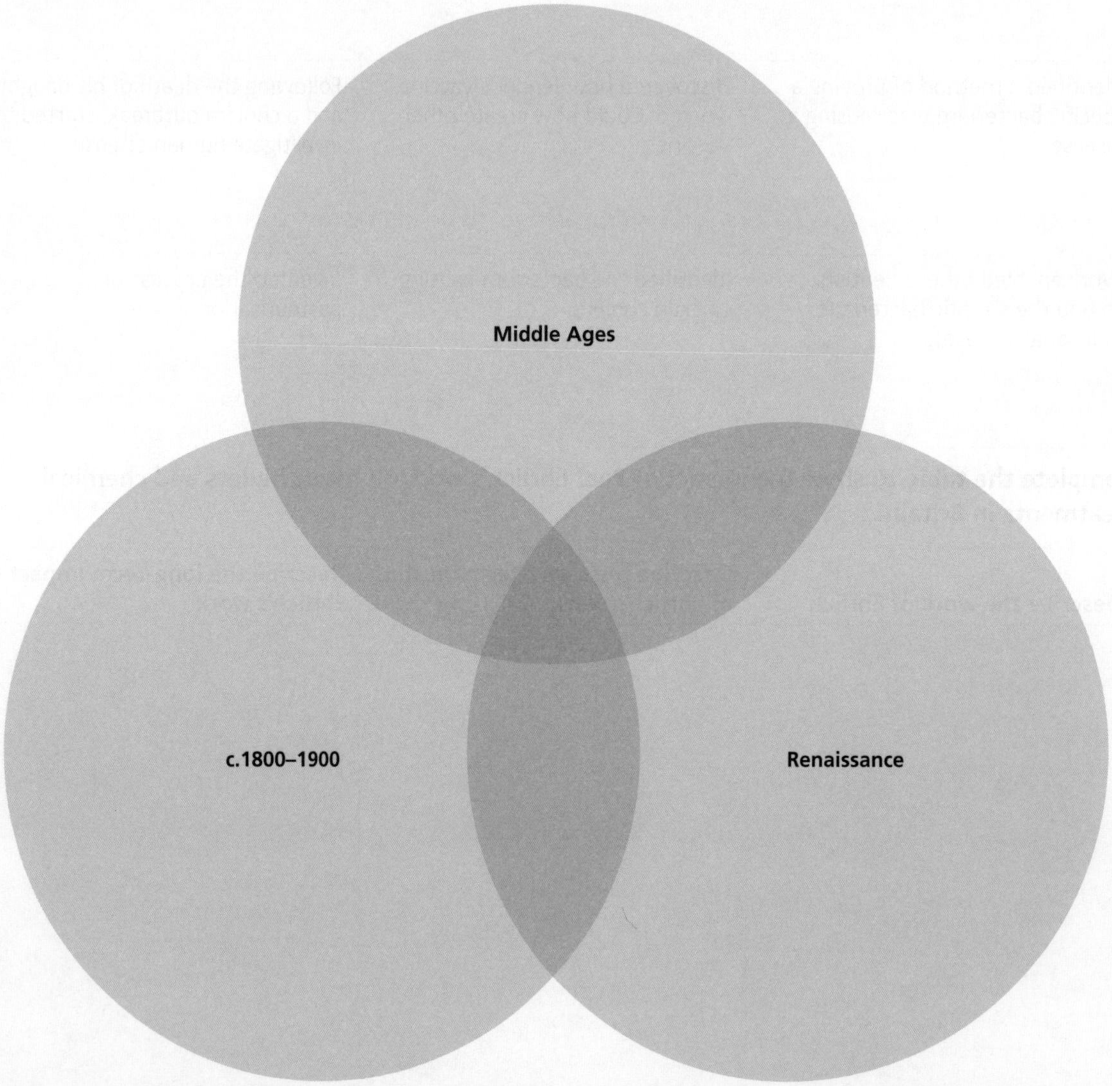

A revolution in surgery

Source E

Simpson and his friends recovering from the effects of chloroform

5 a **Label the key features of Source E.**

b **In which year was Source E created?**

....

c **What is the purpose of Source E?**

....

6 **Write an account of Joseph Lister's work using all the following words:**

- Pasteur's germ theory
- Infection
- Carbolic spray
- Sewage
- Experiment
- Opposition
- Antiseptic

....

....

....

....

....

....

....

....

....

....

....

....

7 **Complete the table to show how the following factors either helped or hindered improvements in surgery during the nineteenth century.**

Factor	Helped or hindered	Explanation
Religion	Hindered	When Simpson discovered chloroform as a method of preventing pain some religious people were opposed as they thought pain was natural and important.
Role of the individual		
Government		

Improvements in public health

8 **Write three sentences with evidence to show that public health had improved by 1900. One has been completed for you as an example.**

1 **A new Food Regulations Act prevented milk being watered down and coloured with chalk powder.**

2 ....

....

3 ....

....

4 ....

....

9 **Use Source F on page 23 to answer the following questions.**

a **When was Source F produced?**

....

b **What was happening at this time?**

....

c **Who produced Source F?**

....

d **Why would the producer publish Source F?**

....

....

Source F

A cartoon published in *The Times* newspaper

10 a **Complete the table to show the stages used by John Snow to prove that cholera was caused by infected water. The first and last have been completed to help you.**

b **Highlight evidence of careful investigation helping to identify the link between dirty water and cholera.**

1849: Snow published a book arguing that cholera was spread by dirty water.
A nearby cesspit was found to have been leaking dirty water into the water supply.

11 **Add at least three statements to the Venn diagram to show similarities and differences between the Black Death 1348–49 and cholera outbreaks during the mid-nineteenth century. Think about the epidemics and their impact.**

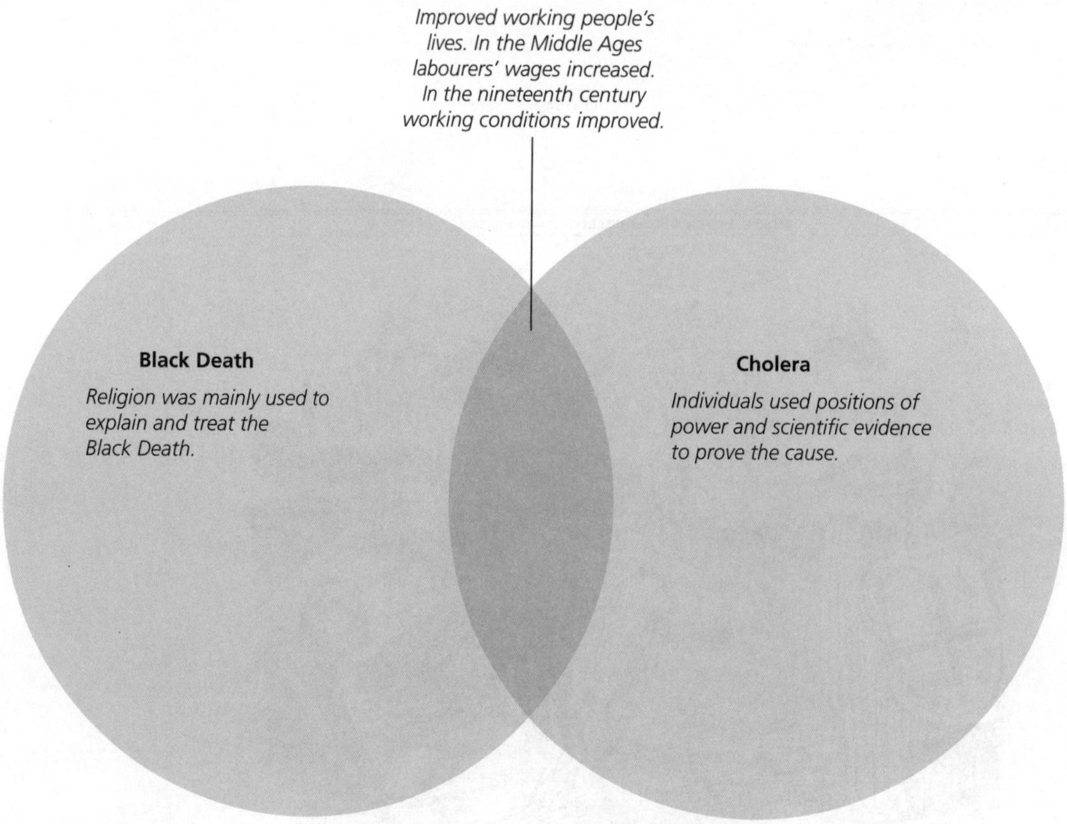

12 **Read the following paragraph on Chadwick's work on public health.**

Colour code the text:

- **Use green for the positive outcomes of the report.**
- **Use pink for the limitations of the report.**

Edwin Chadwick was Secretary to the Poor Law Commissioners. In 1842 he wrote a 'Report on the Sanitary Conditions of the Labouring Population'. It linked poverty to poor living standards and ill health. It encouraged the government and convinced many people of the need for public health reform. It led to the creation of the Health of Towns Association in 1844. However, it was another five years until legislation was passed. The Public Health Act 1848 encouraged local councils to take action but it was voluntary and many did nothing. The impact of Chadwick's report was short. By 1850 Chadwick had little influence.

13 **Draw lines to match each statement about public health reform to the correct individual.**

Individual	Public health reform
William Farr	Studied diseases linked to poverty and produced papers using his findings. They included specific examples and data. His work was used by Chadwick to support his argument for improvements in public health.
Thomas Southwood Smith	Established the 'ragged school' in East London. It provided a basic education for destitute children. He later created other places that offered training in skills and helped find jobs in local areas. A series of homes was opened and a fund created to help children visit the countryside.
Dr Thomas John Barnardo	Introduced compulsory registration of births, marriages and deaths in 1837. This made local authorities more aware of health problems.

14 a Rank the following individuals in order of the importance you believe each had in public health reform.

Individual	Rank order
William Farr	
Thomas Southwood Smith	
Edwin Chadwick	
Dr Thomas John Barnardo	

b Explain your reason for the individual you placed at the top.

15 Use all the following key words to write a short paragraph describing the 1848 Public Health Act.

- **Encourage**
- **Voluntary**
- **Local Boards of Health**
- **Medical Officer**
- **Central Board of Health**

16 a Read the following paragraph about the 1875 Public Health Act. Highlight all the inaccurate statements.

b Re-write all the inaccurate statements on the lines below.

In 1856 the Public Health Act was passed. It set out all the legal requirements local councils had to meet on public health. It was a voluntary act. Local authorities had to appoint at least ten Medical Officers to oversee public health and medicine in their local area. Their roles included keeping sewers in good condition and covered, providing fresh water and collecting rubbish. However, they did not have to regulate slaughterhouses or food.

17 **Draw lines to match each area to the correct public health legislation.**

Area	Public health legislation
Housing	1802 onwards Factory Acts
Working conditions	1853 compulsory vaccination for smallpox
Food	1876 food regulations covering shops
Medicine	1876 building regulations

18 **Why did public health start to improve during the nineteenth century?**

a **For each factor in the table, add evidence of how it helped improve public health during the nineteenth century. One has been completed for you as an example.**

Factor	How it helped improve public health
Government	
Changing attitudes	Weakening of laissez-faire. Government had a role to play in society and everyday lives.
Science and technology	
Cholera outbreaks	
Edwin Chadwick's report	
John Snow and the Broad Street Pump	
Franchise change 1867 – all working men in towns given the right to vote for the first time	
Germ theory, 1861	
Improved communications	

b Copy and complete the diamond nine to show the importance of these factors.

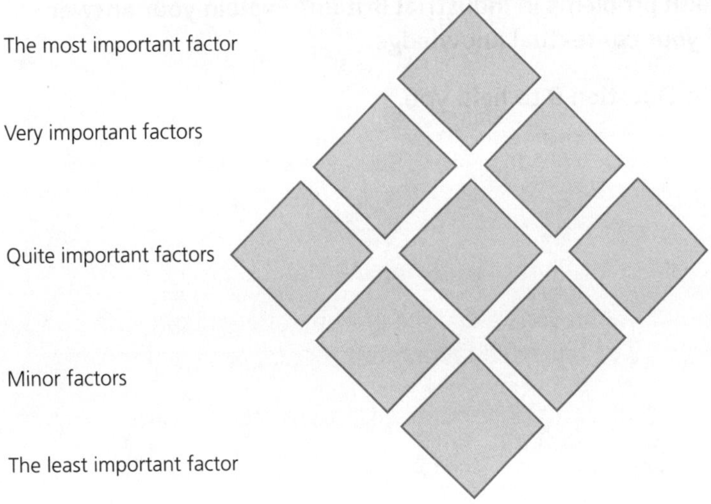

Exam-style questions

19 How useful is Source E (refer to Question 5 on page 21) to a historian studying the work of James Simpson?

Explain your answer using Source E and your contextual knowledge. 10 8 marks

Hint: Use your answers to Question 5 to help you plan your answer.

....

....

....

....

....

....

....

....

....

....

....

....

....

....

....

....

20 **How useful is Source F (refer to Question 9 on page 23) to a historian studying public health problems in industrial Britain? Explain your answer using Source F and your contextual knowledge.** 10 8 marks

Use your answers to Question 9 to help you.

21 **Explain the significance of Joseph Lister's work in the development of surgery.** 10 8 marks

22 **Explain the significance of the British government in the development of public health during the nineteenth century.** 10 **8 marks**

23 **Explain the significance of Robert Koch's work in the development of medicine.** 10 **8 marks**

24 Compare John Hunter's methods of advancing surgery with Joseph Lister's surgery. In what ways were they similar? Explain your answer with reference to both individuals.

10 **8 marks**

Tips for answering 'Compare...' questions:

- Make a big point – what both individuals did or what they did differently, or what was similar/different about the eras.
- Follow with a specific example for each individual or era.
- Make sure you give two or three examples of similarities or differences.

25 Compare public health provision during the nineteenth century with that during the Middle Ages.

In what ways were they similar? Explain your answer with reference to both eras.

10 **8 marks**

26 **Compare everyday treatments and remedies used during the nineteenth century with those used during the Renaissance.**

In what ways were they similar? Explain your answer with reference to both eras.

10 **8 marks**

Modern medicine

Modern treatment of disease

1 **Correct the spellings of the key words listed below.**

Misspelt word	Correct spelling
Disaese	
Treetment	
Farmaceutical	
Acupuntur	
Surjery	
Trasfussion	
Goverment	
Reformm	

2 a **Draw lines to match each date in the table with the correct event in the discovery and development of penicillin.**

b **Colour code evidence of the following in helping the development of penicillin.**

- **Use yellow for the role of government.**
- **Use blue for the role of individuals.**
- **Use green for the role of science.**
- **Use pink for the role of war.**

Date	Event
1880s	Alexander Fleming rediscovered the properties of penicillin.
1928	First test of penicillin on a human; it was a success.
1937	Joseph Lister used penicillin to treat an infected wound, but did not realise its benefits.
1940	Florey and Chain proved the potential of penicillin by experimenting on mice.
1941	American and British governments fund the production of penicillin to treat their soldiers fighting in the Second World War.
1942	Penicillin is a common form of treatment.
Today	Florey and Chain researched penicillin after reading Fleming's article on it.

3 **Use all the following key words to write a short paragraph about the development of the pharmaceutical industry since 1945.**

- **Free samples**
- **Poor drug trials**
- **Thalidomide**
- **Testing**
- **Regulation**
- **Wealthy industry**

....

....

....

....

....

....

4 a **Define 'alternative treatments'.**

....

....

b **List four examples of alternative treatments.**

1 ....

....

....

2 ....

....

....

3 ....

....

....

4 ....

....

....

c **Star the alternative treatments in your list that are recognised by the British Medical Association.**

5 **Briefly explain why alternative treatments have become more popular.**

....

....

....

....

....

....

....

....

....

....

....

....

....

....

The impact of war and technology on surgery

6 **Complete the table to show improvements in surgery in the nineteenth and twentieth centuries.**

Improvement	Discovery or development	Impact of war
X-rays	Wilhelm Röntgen discovered X-rays when carrying out experiments.	Increased in use during the First World War as surgeons needed to locate bullets. X-rays were introduced in all major hospitals on the Western Front.
Blood transfusions	Used from 1800s with different amounts of success. Karl Landsteiner then discovered blood groups, making transfusions possible.	
Plastic surgery		The treatment of injuries resulting from gunfire, explosions and burns in the First and Second World Wars led to major advances in plastic surgery.

7 **Complete the spider diagram to show how war brings about advances in surgery. One example has been completed for you.**

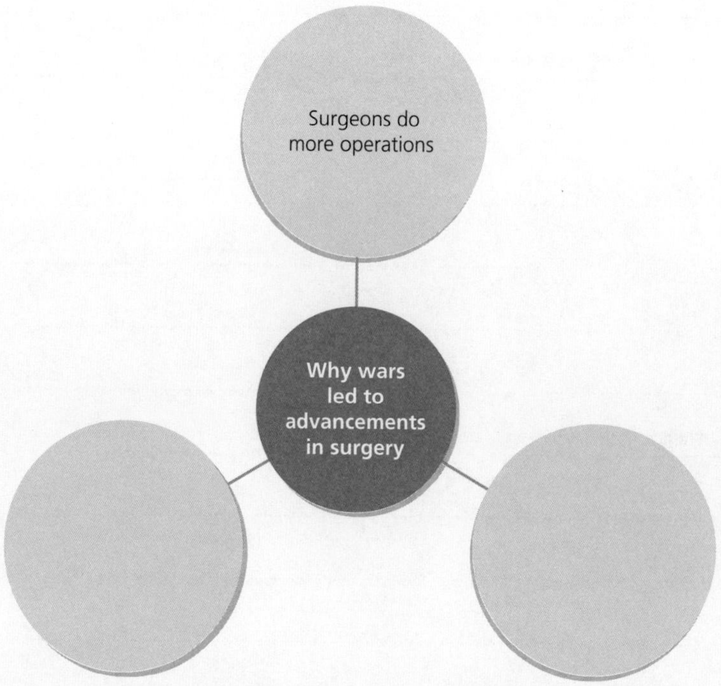

8 Briefly describe each of the modern surgical methods.

Modern surgical method	Brief description
Transplant surgery	
Laser	
Radiation therapy	
Keyhole surgery	

9 Give an example of how each of the following factors influenced change in surgery during the twentieth century.

- War

....

....

....

- Technology

....

....

....

- Individuals

....

....

....

- Improvements in drugs

....

....

....

Modern public health

⑩ **Based on your own opinion, rank the impact of the ideas and work of the individuals listed below on the progress of modern public health in Britain. Give specific reasons and the short- and long-term impacts.**

Individuals:

- **Charles Booth**
- **Seebohm Rowntree**
- **Maud Pember Reeves**
- **William Beveridge**

Rank order	Name	Reason
1		
2		
3		
4		

⑪ a **Tick to show if each statement about the Liberal Government social reforms in the early 1900s is true or false.**

Statement	True	False
In 1906 the government introduced free school meals.		
The Old Age Pensions Act was passed in 1900.		
The Housing and Town Planning Act made building back-to-back houses illegal.		
The Labour Exchanges Act 1909 allowed people to swap jobs with each other.		
The National Insurance Act 1911 introduced compensation for all accidents.		

b **Re-write each false statement to make it correct.**

....

....

....

....

....

....

....

....

12 **'The Liberal Reforms of 1906–14 had limited impact.'**

Write three sentences with evidence that proves this statement. One has been completed for you as an example.

1 **Pensions were introduced for the over-70s, but the average life expectancy was 50.**

2 ....

....

....

3 ....

....

....

4 ....

....

....

13 **Which war? Tick the appropriate box to link each impact of war to either the First or Second World War or to both.**

Impact of war	**First World War**	**Second World War**
Housing Act. Promised 'homes fit for heroes'. Local councils had to provide new homes for soldiers. A quarter of a million new homes were built.		
Slum clearance.		
Children were evacuated to the countryside. The middle class were shocked by their poor state of health – calls for improved health system.		
A report published during the war highlighted poor standards of health and the need for government action.		
Government involvement in everyday life had been accepted during the war. People had higher expectations of the government.		

14 a **Read the following paragraph on the Beveridge Report. Highlight all the inaccuracies.**

b **Re-write all the inaccurate statements on the lines below.**

In 1945 civil servant William Beveridge put forward his ideas on the creation of a free healthcare system in Britain. It was known as the William report. In it he suggested the replacement of the National Insurance scheme introduced by the Conservatives in 1911 with a new welfare system. It was designed to prevent people falling below a minimum level of poverty. To achieve this Beveridge identified ten issues that needed to be tackled in Britain and France.

....

....

....

....

....

....

....

15 **List five services provided by the NHS in 1948.**

1 ....

2 ....

3 ....

4 ....

5 ....

16 **Complete the spider diagram to show opposition to the creation of the NHS.**

In the blank shapes add 'big points'. For each big point add one or two specific pieces of evidence as shown in the example.

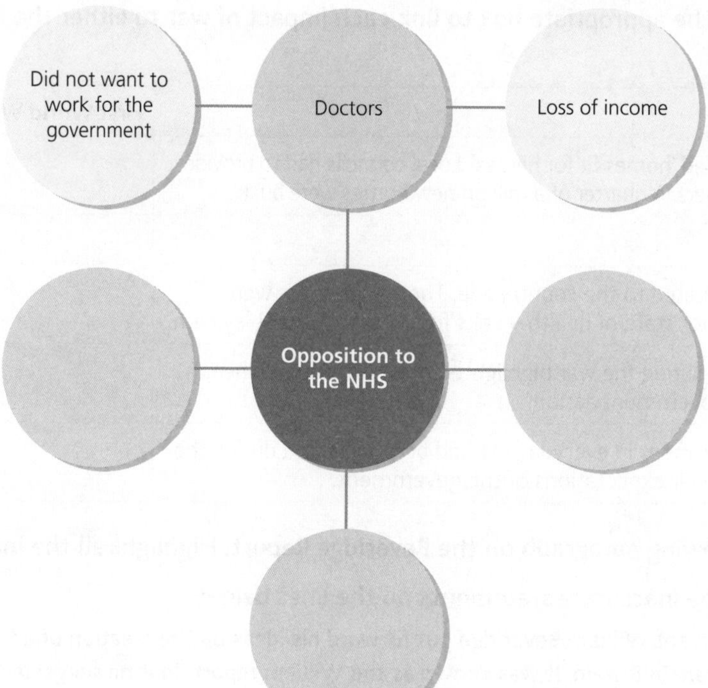

17 **Circle or highlight the statements that are problems faced by the NHS today.**

Cost	**Growth of private healthcare**	**Austerity**	**War**	**Lack of technology**
The cost of running the NHS is continually growing due to an ageing population and increasing number of drugs.	As people grow wealthier they rely less on the NHS.	Demands placed on the NHS to survive on a minimal budget.	The high number of war casualties makes it hard to manage civilians and soldiers.	No investment in technology and science by private companies.

18 **Choose one of the healthcare campaigns below and briefly describe it.**

- **Change4Life**
- **Smokefree programme**

....

....

....

....

....

....

....

....

19 **Define the following key terminology.**

Key terminology	Definition
Austerity	
Compulsory	
Holistic medicine	
Malnourishment	
Welfare state	
Antibiotic	
Gene	
Medical officer	

20 **List three of the major killers in the twentieth century.**

1 ....

2 ....

3 ....

Exam-style questions

Source G

The development of penicillin

21 **How useful is Source G to a historian studying the development of penicillin? Explain your answer using Source G and your contextual knowledge.**

10 | 8 marks

Use your answers to Question 2 on page 32 to help you.

22 **Explain the significance of the Boer War in the advancement of public health in the twentieth century.** 10 8 marks

23 **Explain the significance of vaccination in the development of medicine in Britain.** 10 8 marks

Hint: Think about Jenner and his work on cowpox, as well as the impact of modern day vaccination.

24 **Explain the significance of war in the development of surgery during the twentieth century.**

10 **8 marks**

25 **Explain the significance of the creation of the National Health Service (NHS) in the advancement of public health in the twentieth century.**

10 **8 marks**

26 **Compare the impact of war on surgery during the Ranaissance and the twentieth century.**

In what ways was it similar? Explain your answer with reference to both eras. 10 8 marks

27 **Compare the legislation on public health in the mid-1800s with the Liberal reforms in the early 1900s.**

In what ways were they similar? Explain your answer with reference to both eras. 10 8 marks

28 **Compare the current single-issue health campaigns with the work of individuals campaigning for public health change in the early 1900s.**

In what ways are they different? Explain your answer with reference to both eras.

10 **8 marks**

29 **Compare public health provision during the late nineteenth century with the second half of the twentieth century.**

In what ways were they different? Explain your answer with reference to both eras.

10 **8 marks**

Practice questions

Exam-style questions

In the Health and the people: c.1000 to the present day examination paper, one question will ask you to make a judgement that spans a significant breadth of time. Now you have completed the revision Workbook, answer the following questions. It is strongly advised that you take a break between each question.

Answer the questions on separate pieces of paper.

1. Has religion been the main factor in hindering the progress of medicine in Britain c.1000 to the present day?

   Explain your answer with reference to religion and other factors. Use examples from your study of Health and the people. 20 16 marks

   Tips for answering essay questions:

   - Use a clear structure for your essay (introduction, factor from the question, second factor, third factor, conclusion).
   - For each factor, assess whether it is the main factor. Explain why, using specific examples.

2. Has the role of the individual been the main factor in helping medicine to progress in Britain?

   Explain your answer with reference to role of the individual and other factors. Use examples from your study of Health and the people. 20 16 marks

3. Have changing attitudes been the main factor in the development of medicine in Britain c.1000 to the present day? Explain your answer with reference to changing attitudes and other factors.

   Use a range of examples from across your study of Health and the people. 20 16 marks

4. Have science and technology been the main factors in helping surgery to progress in Britain from 1500 to present day?

   Explain your answer with reference to science and technology and other factors. Use examples from your study of Health and the people. 20 16 marks

5. Has the work of individuals been the main factor in helping public health to improve in Britain c.1000 to the present day?

   Explain your answer with reference to the work of individuals and other factors. Use examples from your study of Health and the people. 20 16 marks

6. Has the British government been the main factor in the development of medicine in Britain since 1700? Explain your answer with reference to the British government and other factors.

   Use a range of examples from across your study of Health and the people. 20 16 marks

Test yourself on the whole paper

Exam-style questions

The following questions are styled using the four question types from the examination paper. Answer all four in timed examination conditions on a separate piece of paper. It is advised that you spend 50 minutes completing all four questions.

Source H

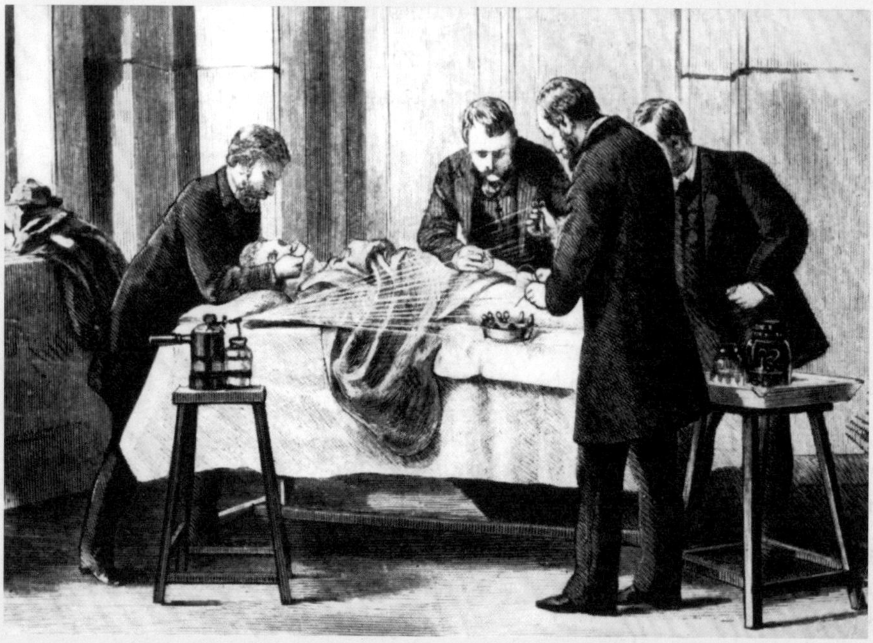

Woodcut of Joseph Lister doing a surgery, 1882

1 How useful is Source H to a historian studying the development of surgery in the late 1800s? Explain your answer using Source H and your contextual knowledge. 10 **8 marks**

2 **Explain the influence of the Church on treatments during the Middle Ages.** 10 **8 marks**

3 **Compare the work and impact of public health reformers in the early 1900s with the work and impact of public reformers 1840–60.**

In what ways were they similar? Explain your answer with reference to both eras. 10 **8 marks**

Answer the following question on a separate piece of paper.

4 **Has chance been the main factor in the development of medicine in Britain since medieval times?**

Explain your answer with reference to chance and other factors.

Use a range of examples from across your study of Health and the people: c.1000 to the present day. 20 **16 marks**

REVISION AND PRACTICE RESOURCES

AQA GCSE (9–1) History

Workbooks

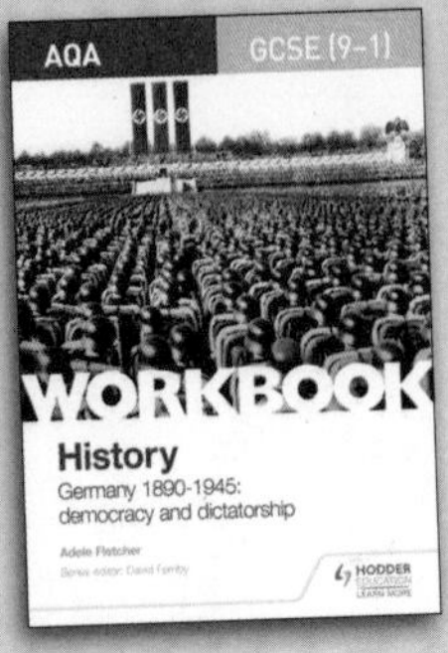

ISBN: 9781510418967

ISBN: 9781510418974

ISBN: 9781510418981

ISBN: 9781510418998

ISBN: 9781510418622

My Revision Notes

ISBN: 9781510404045

Hindsight magazine for GCSE History

Deepen knowledge • Improve skills • Achieve success

Print

eMagazine

Magazine Archive

For more information and/or to order *Hindsight* magazine, visit **www.hoddereducation.co.uk/Magazines**

Find out more and order online at: www.hoddereducation.co.uk/History/GCSE/AQA

Hodder Education, an Hachette UK company, Blenheim Court, George Street, Banbury, Oxfordshire OX16 5BH

Orders

Bookpoint Ltd, 130 Milton Park, Abingdon, Oxfordshire OX14 4SB

tel: 01235 827827

fax: 01235 400401

e-mail: education@bookpoint.co.uk

Lines are open 9.00 a.m.–5.00 p.m., Monday to Saturday, with a 24-hour message answering service. You can also order through the Hodder Education website: www.hoddereducation.co.uk

ISBN 978-1-5104-1897-4

First printed 2018

Impression number 5 4 3 2 1

Year 2022 2021 2020 2019 2018

Cover photo: Haywood Magee/Getty Images. Other photographs reproduced by permission of: **p.7** DEA/A. Dagli Orti/Getty Images; **p.9** Science History Images/Alamy Stock Photo; **p.13** Mary Evans/Everett Collection; **p.17** Mary Evans Picture Library; **p.21** Wellcome Library, London. Wellcome Images; **p.23** World History Archive/Alamy Stock Photo; **p.40** INTERFOTO/Alamy Stock Photo; **p.46** Sammlung Rauch/INTERFOTOMary Evans.

Typeset by Aptara, India

Printed in Spain

Hachette UK's policy is to use papers that are natural, renewable and recyclable products and made from wood grown in sustainable forests. The logging and manufacturing processes are expected to conform to the environmental regulations of the country of origin.

HODDER EDUCATION

t: 01235 827827

e: education@bookpoint.co.uk

w: hoddereducation.co.uk

ISBN 978-1-5104-1897-4

9 781510 418974

MIX
Paper from responsible sources
FSC
www.fsc.org
FSC™ C104740